Surviving You

Audrey Lanford

BookLeaf
Publishing

India | USA | UK

Presentation by *BookLeaf Publishing*

Web: www.bookleafpub.com

E-mail: info@bookleafpub.com

ISBN: 978-93-5744-984-7

First edition 2022

DEDICATION

To W. M., without whom none of this would have been possible.

ACKNOWLEDGEMENT

I am eternally grateful to my former in-laws for their support, to my wonderful therapist who helped me realize my own strength, my mom for believing in me, and my friends on both sides of the country who helped me through some of my darkest times. I would not be here without all of you.

Witchcraft (October 31st)

You cast a spell over me--
A few words and I was yours.
You made promises,
Offered me grandeur,
Made me feel like your savior.
I lost myself in the magic fervor
And we intertwined.

You held me close
As the sweetest blessing
Issued from your lips.
I dedicated myself to you
My own self forgotten
As I became your servant
I dug my nails into the dirt
And befriended sacrifice and misery
Convinced that you were worth it,
That things would be better in time.

No need for a voodoo doll;
You had a puppet.

You became miserly,
Awarding me crumbs of love
As if I was unworthy of more.
You owned me
I despaired

To break the spell
Would be to admit
That everyone who doubted
Us
Was right.

Honeybee

Your honeyed words slide down my throat
Satisfying my appetite for assurance
They sink into my skin, pervading my pores
As you hold me in your arms
Thin and delicate as wire
But a snare all the same

I am the bee you caught in a jar,
Trapped, confused, and alone
Is a flower too much to ask for?
Each one you give me is dry,
Containing too little nectar to sustain me.
I can't produce the honey I want
Because it's all for you

(But you don't need me
You can make your own)

I wait
Until I remember that I have wings
And a stinger.

Imbalance

I cracked open a window
And you broke down the door
I dipped a toe in
And you pulled me into the deep end
I struck a match
And you set off a bomb
I poured you a glass of wine
And you snatched the bottle from my hands
I offered you a dollar
And you stole my wallet
I built you a pedestal
And you demanded a throne.

I asked for a foot
But you gave me an inch
I needed a hand
But you let mine go
I asked for a lantern
But you handed me a light bulb
I asked for sugar
But you gave me salt.
I asked for your insight
But you gave me criticism
I wanted an embrace
But you turned away.

You were too much and not enough.
I was just nothing.

Bottled Up

I found something
And I'm excited to share it
With you, my partner
I tell you how much it means to me
Or how I want to learn more about it

You listen politely
Your response is a veiled barb,
A needle seeking the smallest vulnerability
I talk about my passion again later
But the words soon die in my throat
As you turn away.

I discover something else
And I want to share it
With you, my partner
But I hesitate even as I approach you
I mention my discovery
"That's nice," you reply,
Not looking at me
I take the sting reluctantly
As I retreat, defeated.

Something important happened to me
And I'd like to share it

With you, my partner.
But you've been in a bad mood today
Every word you've said
Has been a stab in my chest
I try to tell you anyway

Why are you laughing?

Eggshells

I have to tell you something.
It's important.
I need to communicate this.
But how will you take it?
There's a chance it will be fine
But there's a greater chance that it won't.
It's so silly,
Such a small thing,
But even the small things can spell doom--
At least with you.
A smile, "I want to talk to you about
something."
I hold my breath--
How can I phrase this so that you won't be
angry?
Please don't take this the wrong way,
Please don't--

Crocodile Tears

I never thought it was possible
To mean crocodile tears
But there you are,
Sitting in your pond,
Wailing at the top of your lungs.
You demand more,
To be fed more,
To be prioritized over more important matters,
To be admired for your predatory strength.
You're always chewing through
The ropes around your jaws
Because nothing is enough to satiate you.
I reach into your mouth
(Like the fool I am)
To try to rescue the innocent little creatures
Caught among your teeth.
As my arm disappears
Into your gaping maw,
You begin your death roll,
Pulling me into the muck--
And I'm stuck.
My blood
Colors the mud
And I fear it's too late for me now.

Sleeping In

By 10:30 AM,
You're already mad at me
Because I'm off work today and I slept in
And you've been up for hours without your
favorite toy

By 11:30 AM,
You've torn down my self-esteem
Because I'm home, and I'm here
And you're bored

By 2:00 PM,
You've made me cry twice
Because I can't do anything right
And you're restless and frustrated

By 5:00 PM,
I'm wishing I'd worked today
Because you've given me shit when I exercised
agency
And my restful day has already been wasted

By 7:30 PM,
We've gotten into an argument that's lasted since
dinner

Because I dared to stand up to you
And you hate when I have any power

By 9:30 PM,
You've gone to bed
Because you're depressed (or so you say)
And I'm relieved you're gone

By 11:30 PM,
I'm drunk off my ass
And it's the first time
I've felt good
All day.

Supply and Demand

In this economy of give and take
You are the upper crust
I exist to provide for you,
To feed you from my own plate
Because yours empties so quickly

You dangle your wealth above my head
Even as you siphon it from my accounts
"Look what you gave me,"
You seem to say
Before demanding more

It'll never be enough, will it?
When you bleed me dry
And throw away my husk,
You'll find some other way
To get your fix

I had much to give
But you had no right to take it all.

Hating myself

I began to hate
The sound of my name
Because you spit it like venom
I began to hate
Being called beautiful
Because it was a cop-out
I began to hate
The sound of my tears
Because I heard it so often
I began to hate
Myself
Because you made me believe I should.

The Gallows

I resigned myself to the rest of my life
As a prisoner in a cell you built just for me
With a small window near the ceiling,
Too far away for the sun to touch my face.

I survived on scraps of love and crumbs of
appreciation.
Though deprived of affection and warmth,
I told myself,
"I am happy here."

Nourishment came more infrequently
And I choked on the words you fed me.
I clung desperately to the hope
That I would see light again.

But you tightened my shackles
And swallowed the key,
Tied a noose gently around my neck
So I'd get used to the sensation.

When the time came for you to pull the lever
I slipped out of my bindings
I jumped off the platform
And I ran toward the sun.

Disillusionment

Instant attraction--
Magnetic, fascinating
A stranger who has known me for years
(Or so it seems)

Meeting you was like answering a question I
never asked
A gold-plated treasure in a dusty attic
Better hold onto it--
It might be worth something

Meticulously setting up the story
The characters ever static
Though the scenery changed
We were the one constant

It was us against the world
And then it was just us
You against me, and me against the problem
Never accepting that the problem was you

Meticulously setting up the joke
Stealing pieces of me
Taking more than you were freely given
The punchline:

Me
Alone

Who am I now?
How much better am I without you?
Infinitely, infinitely--
As I curse your name to the skies.

Mirror

What do you see in the mirror?
Let me hold it for you.
Look into your own eyes--
What do you see there?
What is hiding within the icy blue depths?
Try to strike a match in that darkness--
How long does it take to go out?
Does it survive and burn to your fingertips,
Or does it flicker out instantly?
Either way, it's not bright enough.

Try to delve deeper
And find a frigid body of water--
Narrow as a puddle, but deep as an ocean
That claws at your clothes
And pulls you down, down
To insidious caverns where your motivations
brood
And where your prey languishes,
Chained to the walls.

Look at the mirror again
And now it reflects you,
Turns you into an impassable maze.
The further you proceed,

The more lost you become
Until you're trapped within yourself.
You scream, shattering the mirrors.
They reform and the cycle repeats.

You kept me locked away,
And each time I tried to navigate the maze,
I gave up
Or you threw me back into my prison.

Now what do you see in the mirror?
Do you see someone worth loving?
Or do you see nothing at all
Because nothing exists outside of yourself?
Can you touch another person without taking
them hostage?
Are you strong enough to love anyone at all?

You see your own emptiness
In the mirror,
In your glasses,
In the water you drink.
No matter the lens,
You look only for yourself.
Keep those chains oiled, Narcissus,
Or you may never have more than your
reflection.

Under the Influence

Three rights make a left
They also make you dizzy
Which way is up?
Which way is down?
How many times can I turn around?

Make up your mind
Tell me the truth
Can we move forward
Or is it time to part?
How many times will you break my heart?

The world is not a simple thing
However badly you wish it were
Are you strong enough to accept that
Or is it too hard for you?
How will you ever make it through?

Love is intoxicating
Blended with resentment, divine
Why do we cling to the misery?
Is it because we still have hope?
Are we just the punchline to a cosmic joke?

I lived so long with you in my veins

Cirrhotic, shaking with stress
Do you know who you are without me?
How long has it really been over?
What life will I have now that I am sober?

Grapefruit (I should have listened)

The internet told me
To stay away from grapefruit
Because it could butt heads with my meds
And lead to internal bleeding
And brain damage
My best friend told me
I wasn't missing much

My mother told me
To stay away from strangers
Because they could take hold of my soul
And tear it to pieces
And break my heart
My father told me
Not to listen to her

Your mother told me
To be careful with you
Because you play games that drain
And use others as pawns
And leave them in pain
My friends told me

You were a mistake

You were a mistake
You are a stranger
I have tasted you--
Bitter, sour, yet somehow
Bland
I've beaten you at your own game
But I should have listened

I know what I'm missing
And it's not much.

Planned Obsolescence (It looks like the end)

Radio silence
For an entire day
A total breakdown
In communications and operations
Is the program malfunctioning
Or was it flawed to begin with?
We drift in silence on different planets
Strategizing, preparing for the worst
I bide my time and grit my teeth
Slowly inhale through the stalemate
It lasts for hours
Then, finally, a blip on the radar
As you enter orbit
You seat yourself on the couch,
Thousands of light years away
You train your laser on me
As if I'm the enemy
I try to negotiate
As if there's anything here worth negotiating for
But as your finger rests on the trigger,

I know what's coming
I face the inevitable
It looks like the end.

Your greatest opponent is yourself

You are musical chairs.
You are a slinky falling down the stairs.
The music will stop eventually,
And the stairs will end someday.
Who will have a place to sit?
Who will be there at the bottom to pick you up?
How many chairs are left?
How long will you fall on your head?
Your problem is that
You remove the chairs
And throw yourself down the stairs.
When someone falls,
And the staircase concludes,
The game is over.
Have you really won,
Or has everyone else gotten bored
And given up on you?
Because you don't play fair.
Keep removing chairs
And throwing yourself down the stairs
Because in the end,
Your playmates will find games with fairer rules

And you'll switch to solitaire:
A game which,
Sometimes,
Even you can't win.

Adrift

What happens to the world
When it changes from grayscale to black?
Where do your favorite things go?
Where is home?
Why did this happen to you?

I float in the void,
Searching for something to hold onto,
Purchase on anything that isn't floating with me
There are no stars,
No bright creatures to illuminate this abyss

I am in a vacuum
The air sucked from my lungs
Adrift in nothingness
Alone with my circular, racing thoughts
And yet

I can breathe
As though a vice has been removed
A light appears on the horizon
Warmth begins to drive away the cold
And soon a hand touches me

I am pulled back to the home I know
Filled with love and brightness
Remembering life in color,
I smile again
But the darkness lingers in me yet.

Some habits die easily

Loving you was easy at first
Like a habit I wanted to get into
I loved you immediately, automatically
Everything I saw, I treasured
Until you consumed me

Loving you became reflexive
Giving you my all was instinctive
Then it became mechanical,
Thoughtless as breathing
I defended you without hesitation

Now I look at everything I loved about you
And I see through the illusion
And I wonder
How anyone could love you
And I can't remember why I did.

Inhale

My skin hungers for a touch of sunlight
My lungs cry out for oxygen
My heart staggers beneath the burden of you
And my mind thrashes to loosen your grip

Suddenly, I am thrust into the open
The sunlight blinds me
Even as my skin welcomes it
It takes a week to stop shivering

The cold darkness has made its home
In my bones
My broken heart
Continues to beat the odds

My lips remember how to move
My voice cracks before it clears
My spine straightens
As your weight lifts from my shoulders

My body rises from the ground,
Pulling my mind up with it
My heart falls into its rhythm
And I inhale the fresh air.

Body of Water

Deep currents swirling beneath a windswept
surface
Creatures bright and dark
Drifting, drifting
Shining corals inhabited by
Dreams, hopes, fears
Her heartbeat steady as the tide
As her breath crashes over me
I wade in slowly
So as not to disturb the sacred ecosystem
Learning the ripples of her ocean
To sail upon the surface will not suffice
I tread water carefully
But I can't resist the siren song
I
Could
Drown
But I don't
Fear
The rip currents
I don't
Fear the trenches
Even if I find myself dashed upon a rocky
shore--
Better than never swimming at all.

I breathe in the warm, salty air
As she welcomes me into her depths.

Lemonade

A step in one direction, I follow
And then I lead
And then it's a march, side-by-side
With a dancing rhythm
Time kept by two beating hearts
A parade route we didn't plan
But still know just the same
Sugar mixed in to make sweet lemonade
A little acidity is healthy
A song on the radio
That comes on just as you think of it
A word you steal from my mind
Before it reaches my lips
A match is struck--
How high will the flame burn?
It dances in your eyes, reflects in mine
Every smile is a ray of sunlight
Every kiss a sip of sweet wine, intoxicating
Arms a sanctuary
A gentle caress replaces words
No need to ask questions
Just instant understanding
Let me swim in your depths,
Find the pearls in your oysters,
The treasure in your shipwrecks

Let me taste the chocolate in your eyes
And relish the music in your laugh
My name is a symphony on your tongue
Though it was once a dirge on another's
I want your sugar
I want your sour
I want to refresh you as you refresh me--
A cool plunge on a summer day.